Vocabulary and Study Guide

family

I. Read these sentences. Put a circle around the word **family** in each sentence.

Your family can help you.

You can help your family.

2. Draw a picture to show what you do to help your family.

D1277079

Practice Book
1
Use with *School and Family*, pp. 26–29

Name _____ Date _____

Skillbuilder: Read a Calendar

Teacher Directed Use the calendar to answer the questions below.

FEBRUARY

Sunday	Monday	Tuesday	Wednesday	Thursday	Friday	Saturday
						1
2	3	4	5	6	7	8
9	10	11	12	13	14 Valentine's Day	15
16	17 Presidents' Day	18	19	20	21	22
23	24	25	26	27	28	29

Practice the Skill

1. What special day is February 17th?

_____

2. Color Valentine's Day red.

Name _____ Date _____

Vocabulary and Study Guide

job

Read the word in the box. Write one word to finish each sentence.
Then draw a line to the matching picture.

1. Ann does a _____
at school.

2. Ann does a _____
at home.

3. What is your favorite job at school or at home?

_____

_____

On a sheet of paper, draw a picture of yourself doing
the job.

Practice Book
3   **Use with *School and Family*, pp. 36–39**

Name _____ Date _____

Skillbuilder: Compare Pictures and Maps

Teacher Directed Use the picture to follow the directions below.

Practice the Skill

1. Draw a map of the place in the photograph.

   Include buildings and roads in your map.

Vocabulary and Study Guide

leader	rule

Read the words in the box. Write one word to finish
each sentence.

1. A teacher is the _____
of a class.

2. A leader can make a _____
to keep people safe.

3. What is one rule you have to follow in your
school? On a sheet of paper, draw a picture of
yourself following the rule.

_____

_____

_____

_____

Name _____ Date _____

Skillbuilder: Read a Map Key

Teacher Directed Use the map and the map key to follow the directions.

Neighborhood Map

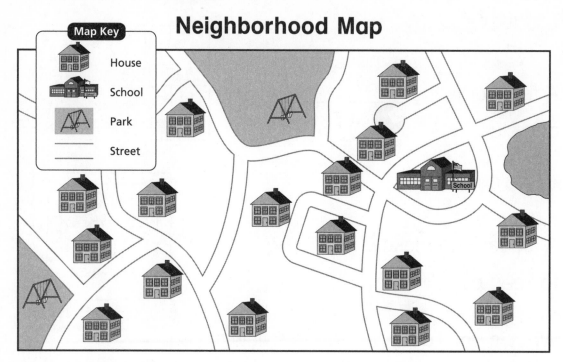

Map Key

House

School

Park

Street

Practice the Skill

1. Find the symbol for School on the map key. Color it blue.

2. Find the School on the map. Color it blue.

3. Put an X on one house. Imagine you live there. Draw the route you would take to get to school.

6

Use with *School and Family*, pp. 52–53

Vocabulary and Study Guide

community

1. Read these sentences. Put a circle around the word **community** in each sentence.

We live and work in a community.

A community has helpers to take care of people and places.

2. Here is a community helper. Draw two more helpers from your community.

Practice Book

7

Use with *School and Family,* **pp. 54–57**

Name _____ Date _____

Vocabulary and Study Guide

country

Read the word in the box. Write a word to finish the sentence.

1. Roberto moved to the United States

   from another _____. He

   brought his favorite music.

2. Draw a picture of yourself showing a new classmate around your school.

Use with *School and Family*, pp. 60–63

Vocabulary and Study Guide

ocean	continent

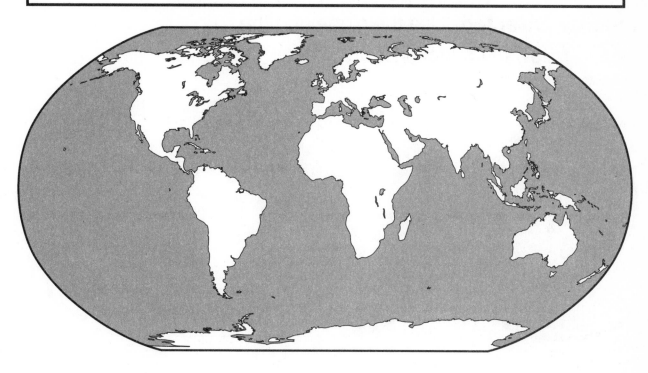

1. Find an ocean on the map and draw an **O** on it.

Find a continent and draw a **C** on it.

2. What are two things you learned about oceans?

_____

_____

Use with *School and Family*, pp. 74–77

Name _____ Date _____

Skillbuilder: Compare Globes and Maps

Teacher Directed Use the globe and the map to follow the directions.

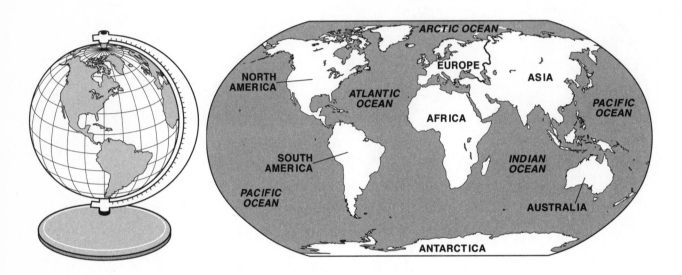

Practice the Skill

1. Find the land areas on the globe and on the map. Color them green.

2. Find the water areas on the globe and on the map. Color them blue.

Name _____ Date _____

Vocabulary and Study Guide

1. Draw a line from the word to the picture of it.

mountain   **plain**   **river**   **lake**

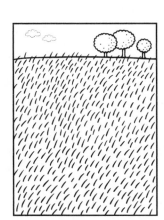  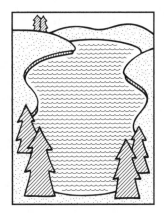 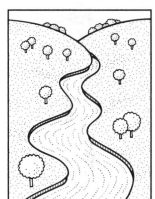

2. Look at the four words again. Put each word under the right heading.

LAND	WATER

Use with *School and Family,* **pp. 82–85**

Vocabulary and Study Guide

1. Use the words in the box to fill in the blanks.

> natural resource

Something in nature that people use is a

_____ .

Water is one kind of _____ .

Soil is another kind of _____ .

2. Draw pictures of two natural resources.

Skillbuilder: Read a Chart

Teacher Directed Use the chart to answer the questions below.

Natural Resources	
Can Be Replaced	**Cannot Be Replaced**
wood from trees	oil for fuel
food from plants	metals
wool from sheep	coal

Practice the Skill

1. What is the title of the chart?

_____

2. Which resource can be replaced, wool or coal?

_____

Name _____ Date _____

Vocabulary and Study Guide

weather	season

1. Draw a line from the word to its meaning.

weather a time of the year

season what it is like outside

2. Circle the picture that shows a season. Put an X on the picture that shows weather. Then draw a picture of your favorite season in the box below.

Fall

Rain

Name _____ Date _____

Vocabulary and Study Guide

Read the clues. Use the words in the box to write the answers.

city	town	suburb

1. It has many people and buildings. _____

2. It is close to a city. _____

3. It has fewer people and streets. _____

Circle the answer.

4. What is this? Circle the answer.

city   suburb   town

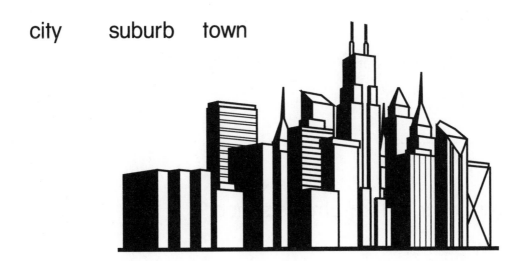

Name _____ Date _____

Skillbuilder: Find Near and Far

Teacher Directed Use the map and the map key to answer the questions.

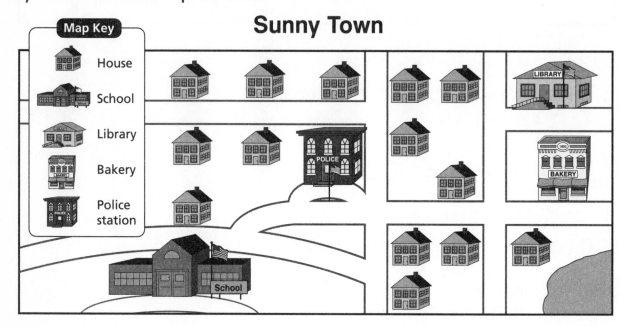

Practice the Skill

1. Is the bakery near or far from the library?

_____

2. Is the library near or far from the school?

_____

Vocabulary and Study Guide

state	citizen

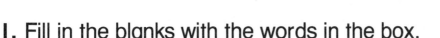

1. Fill in the blanks with the words in the box.

Mark lives in the _____ of Florida.

Mark is a _____ of that state.

2. Circle the word that does NOT belong.

A citizen belongs to a

community   state   country   ocean

3. Write one fact you learned about one of the states.

_____

_____

_____

Vocabulary and Study Guide

neighbors

The map shows that Canada and Mexico are neighbors of the United States.

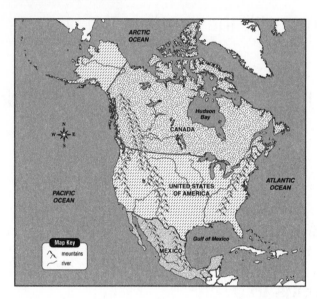

1. Draw a circle around our neighbors to the north. Draw a square around our neighbors to the south.

2. Why are Mexico and Canada neighbors of our country? Circle the correct answer.

    A. We like each other.

    B. We live near each other.

    C. We like to play the same kind of sports games.

    D. We have the same kind of weather.

Practice Book
18 Use with *School and Family,* pp. 116–119

Name _____ Date _____

Vocabulary and Study Guide

needs	scarcity	wants

I. Which picture shows needs and which picture
shows wants? Write the answer under the picture.

_____   _____

2. Circle the word that means not having enough
money to buy all of what a family wants.

needs   scarcity   wants

Skillbuilder: Make a Decision

Teacher Directed Look at the picture and read the words. Help the children decide what to do.

Practice the Skill

1. What do the children have to decide?

_____

2. Write about a good choice.

_____

_____

Name _____ Date _____

Vocabulary and Study Guide

| sell | goods | services | volunteers |

Look at the pictures. Circle the correct word.

1. The baker likes to _____ bread.

   buy   sell

2. Jack is selling _____.

   goods   services

3. The class is selling _____.

   goods   services

4. June spends her free time helping at the zoo. She is one of the _____.

   services   volunteers

5. Name one place to buy goods and one place to buy services in your community.

   _____

   _____

   _____

Practice Book
21   **Use with *School and Family*, pp. 138-141**

Vocabulary and Study Guide

1. Find these words in the puzzle. Circle each one.

cost	save

s	a	v	w	d	f
m	l	c	o	s	t
x	l	o	s	y	t
z	s	a	v	e	x
s	d	g	y	q	w

2. Use the words in the box to fill in the blanks.

Pam needed a new bike. She went with her

parents to the bike shop. She saw a bright red

bike. But it _____ more money than she had.

Maybe Pam will _____ her money and buy the

bright red bike. Maybe she will look for a bike that

does not _____ as much. What could Pam do?

Use with *School and Resources*, pp. 144–147

Skillbuilder: Read a Graph

Teacher Directed Use the graph to answer the questions.

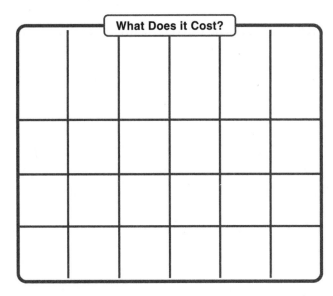

What Does it Cost?

Practice the Skill

1. Which foods cost three dollars each?

_____

2. Which food costs less, the milk or the bananas?

_____

3. Which food costs the most?

_____

Name _____ Date _____

Vocabulary and Study Guide

worker	factory

I. Use the words in the box to fill in the blanks.

A person who does a job is a

_____ .

A place where workers use machines to make goods is a

_____ .

2. Some workers make goods. Some workers give services. Circle the picture of the worker giving a service.

Use with *School and Family*, pp. 152–155

Name _____ Date _____

Vocabulary and Study Guide

Read the words in the box.

machine	seller	buyer

1. Look at the picture. Write **S** on the person who is the seller. Write **B** on the person who is the buyer.

2. Draw a picture of a machine that does work for people. Label the picture.

Name _____ Date _____

Skillbuilder: Use a Compass Rose

Teacher Directed Use the map to answer the questions.

States Where Oranges Grow

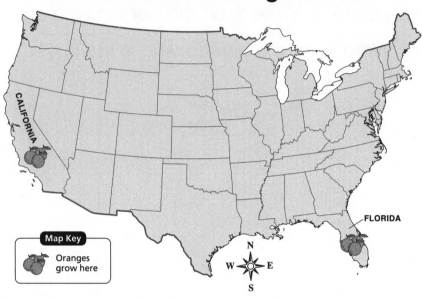

Practice the Skill

1. What directions are on the compass rose?

_____

2. Put your finger on the oranges in Florida. What

direction would you go to get to California?

_____

Name _____ Date _____

Vocabulary and Study Guide

Circle the word from the box that finishes
the sentence.

present	past	history	future

1. This is one way people traveled

in the _____.

   past   present   future

2. This is one way people travel

in the _____.

   past   present   future

3. This is one way people may travel

in the _____.

   past   present   future

Complete this sentence.

4. History _____.

Name _____ Date _____

Skillbuilder: Use a Timeline

Teacher Directed Use the timeline to answer the questions.

Practice the Skill

1. What is the first day shown on the timeline?

_____

2. What did Marco do on the last day?

_____

Practice Book
28 Use with *School and Family,* pp. 182–183

Name _____ Date _____

Vocabulary and Study Guide

I. Use the words in the box to fill in the blanks.

> American Indians

The first people in North America were

_____.

The Chumash and the Cherokee are two groups of

_____.

2. Draw a picture of an American Indian home from the past.

Name _____ Date _____

Vocabulary and Study Guide

settlers	harvest

Read the words in the box. Write one word to complete each sentence.

1. People who come to live in a new place

   are _____.

2. Thanksgiving is a celebration for the

   _____.

3. Draw a picture of a harvest celebration. Your picture can show a celebration from the past or the present.

Name _____ Date _____

Skillbuilder: Solve a Conflict

Teacher Directed Look at the picture and read the words. Then answer the questions.

Practice the Skill

I. What is the conflict?

_____

_____

2. How can the father and son agree on what to do?

_____

_____

Practice Book
31
Use with *School and Family,* pp. 200–201

Vocabulary and Study Guide

Read the word in the box. Write it in the blanks below.

Then draw a line to the picture that matches.

education

1. Long ago, children went to schools with

one room for an _____ .

2. Today, children get an _____

in bigger schools.

3. Look at the pictures below. Which things are from

a school of long ago? Circle them.

 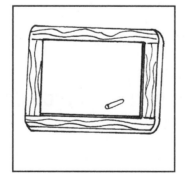 

Name _____ Date _____

Vocabulary and Study Guide

transportation	invention

1. Circle the picture that is NOT a kind of
transportation.

2. Name some inventions that have made
transportation better. Look for clues in the lesson.
Write your answers on the lines.

_____

_____

_____

33   **Use with** *School and Family,* **pp. 208–211**

Name _____ Date _____

Skillbuilder: Compare Points of View

Teacher Directed Read each point of view.
Then answer the questions.

Mira

Nat

Swimming is the best sport.

It makes me strong.

Soccer is the best sport.

I can play it with my friends.

Practice the Skill

1. What is Nat's point of view about sports?

_____

2. Why does Mira think swimming is the best sport?

_____

Practice Book
34
Use with *School and Family,* pp. 214–215

Name _____ Date _____

Vocabulary and Study Guide

communicate	communication

1. Draw a line between the word and its meaning.

communicate   when people share
                               news and ideas

communication   the way people share
                               news and ideas

2. Circle the picture that is NOT a form of communication.

Name _____ Date _____

Vocabulary and Study Guide

law	government

I. Draw a line from the word to its meaning.

law   a group of people chosen

government   to make laws

                           a community rule

2. Circle the sign that shows a law.

Skillbuilder: Express Ideas in Writing

Teacher Directed Read about a rule. Then write clearly to answer the question.

Rules

No running.
Raise your hand.
Put away books and toys.
Talk quietly with a partner.

Practice the Skill

1. Why is it a good idea to follow these rules? Give two reasons that tell why you think so.

_____

_____

Name _____ Date _____

Vocabulary and Study Guide

1. Use the words and the clues to fill in the crossword puzzle.

President	mayor	governor

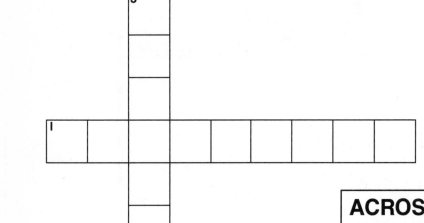

ACROSS

1. the leader of our country
2. the leader of a city or town

DOWN

3. the leader of a state governmnet

2. Fill in the blank to finish the sentence. Use one of the words from the box.

The _____ of our country helps run the government.

38   Use with *School and Family*, pp. 236–241

Vocabulary and Study Guide

| right | responsibility | vote | election |

Complete the vocabulary word by reading the clue
and choosing from the letters.

1. A way to make a choice

_ O T _   M B V E T A S

2. Something you are free to do

_ I _ H _   V E T G R H W

3. A duty to do something

R E _ P _ N S _ B I _ I T _   L O Y I G B S

4. A time when citizens vote for leaders

_ L E _ T _ O N   N V I C L E R

Circle the word that finishes the sentence.

Voting is a citizen's _____.

responsibility   vote   election

Practice Book
39   Use with *School and Family*, pp. 244–247

Name _____ Date _____

Vocabulary and Study Guide

hero

1. Draw a line from the name to the thing that hero did.

Susan B. Anthony

worked to get women the right to vote.

Dr. Martin Luther King, Jr.

helped farm workers get better pay and safer places to work.

Cesar Chavez

spoke against laws unfair to African Americans.

2. What do heroes do when things are hard? Write your answer on the line.

_____

Practice Book

Use with *School and Family,* **pp. 250–253**

Name _____ Date _____

Skillbuilder: Compare Fact and Fiction

Teacher Directed Look at the book covers. Read about the books. Then answer the questions.

Practice the Skill

1. Draw a circle around the book that you think tells facts.

2. How do you know that **Lost on Mars** is a made-up story?

_____

_____

Practice Book
41   Use with *School and Family,* pp. 256–257

Vocabulary and Study Guide

Use the clues and the words in the box to write the answers in the blanks. Then find the words in the puzzle and circle them.

symbol	honor

1. A picture, place, or thing that stands for

something else _____

2. How we treat a symbol to show that our country

is important to us _____

b	s	y	h	d	l
h	o	n	o	v	h
s	y	m	n	k	l
g	h	x	o	n	r
p	y	m	r	o	l
s	y	m	b	o	l

Practice Book
42
Use with *School and Family,* pp. 258–263